A Tini Step Further
Looking Deeper

Martinis Stephens

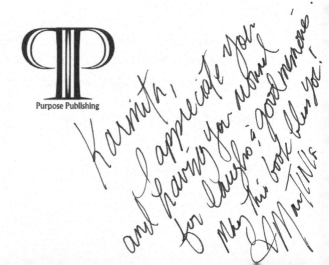

Purpose Publishing

ISBN: 1-7337729-8-3
ISBN-13: 978-1-7337729-8-3

DEDICATION

This book is dedicated to anyone who is dissatisfied with a surface level view of life. It is for those who know that what is seen is not all there is and don't mind looking within, digging deeper, and reflecting on what was and is in order to step into what should be. May God take your hand and guide you as you walk a Tini Step Further into His plans for your life.

CONTENTS

Introduction   1

The Reason. 4

A Tini Step Further. 9

The Swing. 15

Brilliant Mind. 23

My Beautiful Distraction 30

Still. 37

Right This Way 42

Mold Me 51

Deceptive Perspective. 60

Keep Pressin'. 68

Surrender. 75

Beautifully Bold 81

Friend of the Friendless. 89

Kid at Heart 96

To This Day. 105

INTRODUCTION

While it may seem that a first book would be the most difficult of all books to write, as I fully embrace the "writer life," this second book has shown itself to be more tasking. The first time you do something, you may or may not be sure how it's going to go. However, the second time around, you want it to be just as good or better than the first. Comparing the two is not a productive method. I had to tell myself, "Yes, learn from previous mistakes, but focus on the task at hand." The works in this collection were written over a shorter period of time, and during some pretty difficult moments. As always, writing my way through them helped me

1

properly deal with the tough times as I looked to God for guidance and wisdom.

It is my prayer and purpose in sharing this book with you that my struggles, successes, observations, and revelations bless you. I don't want you to just be entertained or enlightened by what you read on these pages. That's not enough. I want you to be stirred to seek God like never before, to be comforted in knowing that you are not alone in your struggles, and to be uplifted as you press on and push through what the enemy attempts to use to hinder your progress.

I truly hope that you take your time and read this book in its entirety. Many people enjoy poems and spoken word. Some have even labeled me a poet. Poetry is used as a tool to help people have ears to hear what I feel led to say. My goal is to exhort and teach, exhortation and teaching being two of the gifts of the Spirit God has given me to help edify the Body of Christ.

As a teacher, it is important to me that you reflect on any information that you receive in order for it to have lasting effects. That being said, the questions and lines in this book are crucial. Flying through the book and omitting the reflection process may have some benefits, but you will miss out on some of what God wants to say and do in, through and for you. May you take in and pour out as you are led to do.

Let the journey begin...

THE REASON

With everything going on outside of me

There's still so much activity within me

Creative juices bubbling

Begging to be released

To set them free would be therapeutic, uplifting

Likewise to those who take in what is poured out

The double blessing of the gifts entrusted to us

To restrain them?

Well, that would be the definition of selfishness and
self-hate

So out of love for you, love for myself, but most of all

Love for the Giver of ALL Gifts

I allow the words to flow out

From my heart, my mind, my life

And into yours

As I pass on what is passed down

In hopes of hearing

"Well done, My Faithful One."

A Tini Step

"The Reason" is my reply to anyone who would ask me why. Why do I write and have the audacity to share what is written? Prior to writing this poem, I had the pleasure of leading a writing Life Group. I thought and prayed about my 'why' as it related to leading the group and as it relates to anything else I choose to do. God has given each of us at least one gift to share and the power of the Holy Spirit gives us the grace to do so. Our gifts are a part of who we are. When we choose not to share them, we withhold a part of ourselves.

The more you allow yourself to flow in whatever gifting God has entrusted to you, the more of your authentic self you are free to be. Also, because the gifts are for glorifying God and for edifying others, withholding them means you're not fully giving God glory AND others are not living life on the level they would be if you released what you're grasping (See Peter 4:10-11).

Reread "The Reason." Then answer the following questions:

1. What are your God-given gifts and talents?

   _____

   _____

   _____

   _____

2. Are you fully using your gifts to help others and bring glory to God? If so, how? If not, what is stopping or hindering you from doing so?

   _____

   _____

   _____

   _____

   _____

3. What can you do to enhance or strengthen your gifts so that you can be more effective?

_____

_____

_____

_____

_____

_____

_____

_____

_____

_____

_____

A TINI STEP FURTHER

To take the next step requires so much

That I don't feel like I have.

All I've known

Looks nothing like where we're going.

But You're saying

"Go."

Take a step deeper, further

Into new territory

To a place I dared to dream of even visiting.

I thought I did this before,

But You laugh and say,

"There's so much more!"

I want to go there.

I really do!

And it's so great to be assured

That I'm going with You.

You with me.

I was just waiting until I was ready,

But is ready a real thing?

Or just some imaginary state

That I reference when I'm being a wuss?

When my legs turn into cooked spaghetti,

Mush,

And the pace is all slow and no steady.

I'm coming, just a second.

Okay.

1... 2... 3...

STEP!

A Tini Step

If you've read *A Tini Step of Faith* (my first book), then you may recall the poem, "Alarm Clock." It could be said that this poem, "A Tini Step Further," is somewhat of a response to the Holy Spirit's awakening and call to rise in "Alarm Clock." We are charged to get out of complacency and rise to the challenge of the life God has for us. I feel like I answered that call, but I've come to notice that there is still **MORE**. We are always being led to go to a greater, higher, and deeper level. We allow ourselves to get comfortable by reminiscing too long on our successes. They were great in the season they occurred, but this is a **NEW** season. God wants to do a **NEW** thing. Bragging about what was won't get you far with God. Your wins should be a springing board off of which you jump from one level to the next.

Reread "A Tini Step Further." Then answer the following questions:

1. Take time to pray and meditate about this: If you were to take the "next step" spiritually, mentally, physically, or financially, what would that mean for you? (This is different for everyone.)

   _____

   _____

   _____

   _____

2. What has been hindering you from taking that step or those steps? If it is fear, fear of what?)

   _____

   _____

   _____

   _____

3. Write out a sincere prayer concerning the steps and hindrances.

_____

_____

_____

_____

_____

_____

_____

_____

_____

_____

_____

_____

_____

THE SWING

From one end to the other

Back and forth

Back and forth

Unstable in all its ways

My mind soars

Then drops

Pros, cons

What ifs and what nots

In a tangled web of thoughts

Caught

I would love to make a quick decision

And know what I want with precision

But my reality is doubled vision

Swinging one way

Then quickly swinging back

While simultaneously being frozen

Procrastinated

Because I'm fascinated

By all the possibilities

Yet all my insecurities

Are screaming within me

I go from "Just Do It!"

To "Don't even think about it!"

All in a matter of minutes

Sometimes seconds

Confusion

A pendulum of mental stress

"Let me think about it."

"I'll let you know."

"I'm still praying about it."

The words I profess

As I digress

Buying time

While wasting the same

Moments I can't get back

Because I'm having a low grade panic attack

Wheels spinning

Going nowhere

Into simple matters

Putting way too much thought or care

Why am I like this?

Recalling that the only way to fight this is to

Follow Peace

Listen to and obey what the Spirit speaks

But then...

Immediate ACTION

Because any delay in movement

Is breeding grounds for distraction

Followed by retraction

How can steps be ordered

If none are ever taken?

So I must get off this swing

Let my mind rest

And my feet move...

This is progress.

A Tini Step

"The Swing" describes what I like to call "**Procrastinating Perfectionism**." It's based on the fear of looking or being wrong and wanting to get things right. But can anything made with humans hands be perfect? It says in the Word of God, "Then God saw everything that He had made, and indeed *it was* very good" (Genesis 1:31 NKJV). It doesn't say "perfect." I spend a considerable amount of energy being frustrated over trying to make things flawless, and they never are. But can I step back, look at what I put my hands to, and say, "It is good"? Good was good enough for God, so where does that leave me?

Because we will never be perfect and are naturally flawed, our work is flawed. We have to be okay knowing this because **perfectionism procrastinates progress and productivity.** While some of the times I've dealt with procrastination have been due to just plain laziness, most of them had to do with perfectionism. I'll start a project after I've thought about all of the aspects surrounding it. This causes me to miss important deadlines or throw something together at the last minute. Surely, this is NOT what God wants. Where's the peace in operating this way? According to Proverbs 16:9, "A man plans his way, but the Lord directs his steps" (NKJV). Take steps, allowing the Lord to adjust them as you go, and you will see success. Perfectionism brings about too much hesitation. Yes, make plans, but also **TAKE STEPS!** God's grace supersedes any and every mistake, misstep, and bad decision you could ever make. Just keep working; keep stepping.

Reread "The Swing." Then answer the following questions:

1. Have you ever dealt with perfectionism? If so, where do you think that it comes from, and how do you feel it has hindered you?

_____

_____

_____

_____

_____

2. What helps you move past perfectionism and get things done?

_____

_____

_____

_____

_____

BRILLIANT MIND

This Brilliant mind of mine

Amazes me at times

It creates masterpieces

And imagines wonders

Yet to be seen by any human eyes

Including my own

Oh Brilliant mind of mine!

Takes me places

My feet have yet to travel

Mountaintops, grassy fields,

Even outer space

Such a Brilliant mind of mine!

It helps me to solve lots of problems

Yet, it has been the cause of the same

Doubt, fear, suspicion,

Anger, hostility...

Too many to name

While I'm awestruck by its wonders

I'm perplexed by its hindrances

How can something so magnificent

Be so dangerous?

The imagination is a wild place

When left unchecked

It multiplies what it's fed

Sights seen with the eyes

Sounds and words heard

Through my ears

Can be stamped in my head

Forever...

It seems

Really gotta watch

What I let get into this thing

Rebooting, cleansing, renewal

These are a must!!!

You are what you eat...

Or is it what you THINK?

A Tini Step

I hear all the time and have even said myself, "Oh, it's no big deal. It's just [insert random activity]." With all this technology and the ability to instantly see and hear any and everything possible, our minds are fed so much junk that we don't even realize is affecting us. We can sing songs from twenty years ago, word for word. I can recall some of my friends' telephone numbers that I used to dial on a phone that had actual buttons. Whatever we repeatedly see, think, hear or do becomes a part of who we are.

Thank goodness Jesus came to make ALL THINGS new (2 Corinthians 5:17). This is just the beginning, though. The Holy Spirit is here for us to help us on our journey. There is a daily renewal process that needs to be carried out in order to maintain a healthy spirit, mind, and body. Ephesians 4 and Romans 12 are two of many times in God's Word that explain the importance of the activities in which we partake. Mental health definitely matters. One way to maintain a healthy mind is by being "mindful" of what you allow to come in it and feed on the Word of God consistently.

Reread "Brilliant Mind." Then answer the following questions:

1. Are there any activities in which you participate that you know are mentally and spiritually unhealthy? Examples: a certain television show you consistently watch or being in a relationship/friendship that you know is not good for you.

    _____

    _____

    _____

    _____

2. How long have you or how often do you participate in these activities?

_____

_____

_____

_____

_____

_____

3. Is there anyone with whom you trust to talk and pray with you concerning these activities? If so, who?

_____

_____

_____

_____

_____

MY BEAUTIFUL DISTRACTION

Such a Beautiful Distraction

How I love to gaze at you

Get lost in what you are

Far away from all I need to do

Responsibilities feel like a weight

So I lay them down to Embrace you

Holding ever so tightly

As productivity begs to replace you

I look away from it

For the sight of tasks bring great sorrow

I lie to myself and simply say,

"I'll get to it all tomorrow."

Such a prideful and foolish statement

For today is all I'm given

And I really can't know for sure

If tomorrow I'll even be living

Yet and still, I waste this time I have

On you and your nothingness

My Beautiful Distraction,

 Can any good ever come from this?

What is it about you

That keeps me mesmerized?

Life wasting away because

I've given up on trying to fight

Giving in to the urges

To give you minute after minute

No room for anything else in life

All because you're in it

Where are the scissors I need to cut

The strings that have us so connected?

There's a pile of **Purpose** next to me

That's been abandoned and neglected

Fading in the background as I blindly focus

On your hypnosis

All my energy poured into your bottomless cup

Of stagnant water, bitter hopelessness

Then guilt, regret, shame

Proceed every session

Beautiful to my eyes...'Tis lies

For you're the cause of my regression

Correction...Confession

It's not you; it's me

I put you first

I'm the one who has to slam the brakes

Put this thing in reverse

Drive as far away from you

As I can possibly get

Father, give me strength; forgive me, Lord

As I refocus and repent

    Amen

A Tini Step

While perfectionism and indecisiveness are major causes of procrastination, "My Beautiful Distraction" points to an equally, if not more, dangerous cause. There are so many ways our attention can be pulled. If I listed distractions, I may or may not include one that is an issue for you, but something electronic, some technological device, whether it be the television, phone, tablet or game system, may very well be on your list. I have to block out time away from my phone and other devices in order to complete projects or take care of other necessary business. There are some people that I have met, however, that easily avoid distractions. They are naturally hyper-focused and self-motivated. God bless them all! Some of us have to pray and really fight against the strong forces that work to pull us away from God's plan for our lives. So what about you? Think about what tends to draw you away from the work you know you're called to do.

Reread "My Beautiful Distraction." Then answer the following questions:

1. What are your biggest, toughest distractions?

_____

_____

_____

_____

2. Knowing that these things delay your progress and hinder your growth, what are some practical ways you can guard yourself against wasted time and unfocused thoughts?

_____

_____

_____

_____

_____

3. I wrote out Psalm 119:15 on an index card and put it where I can easily see it. Look up scriptures about distractions and focus. Find one that stands out for you and write it out

_____

_____

_____

_____

_____

_____

_____

_____

_____

_____

_____

STILL

I sat still

Still enough to hear You

And in that moment

Peace came

As I took a deep breath in

Worries fled

As I exhaled

All I had been holding on to

What I didn't even realize was in my hand

Until

I sat still

Still enough

    To KNOW You

A Tini Step

My initial thought when I wrote this poem was that it's too short to be considered for this book. I kept wanting to add to it so it would be "worthy" of inclusion, but I knew in my heart that it was enough. As stated in the introduction, comparison, even within your own works, can be harmful. As I'm putting everything together, I'm so glad that I included it. The simplicity of it speaks to communing with God. It's just that simple. "Be still and know that I am God" is what we are told in Psalm 46:10 (NKJV).

When life gets as crazy, as stated on previous pages, being still and listening to the "still small voice" (1 Kings 19:11-13) of our Heavenly Father is our path of peace through the chaos. The world can be crashing down all around us while peace that "passes all understanding" (Philippians 4:7) rests within us. This is why it is imperative that we do what is necessary to ask the Holy Spirit to help us fight distractions. The enemy seeks to pull us from a state of being still. Between the fruit of the Spirit (Galatians 5:22-23) and the whole Armor of God (Ephesians 6:10-18), we have what it takes to seek God and no excuse for neglecting time spent sitting in His presence. We read plenty of times where people, Jesus included, went away to pray and get in God's presence. With all that is going on in the world today, shouldn't we be just as willing to do so?

Reread "Still." Then answer the following questions:

1. How often are you still and sitting in the presence of God?

   _____

   _____

   _____

   _____

2. I started writing in my journal first thing every morning as a way to ensure that I began the day sitting still, listening, and praying. What can you do to increase the amount of moments you spend sitting still in His presence?

_____

_____

_____

_____

_____

_____

_____

_____

_____

_____

RIGHT THIS WAY

One turn towards You

All it takes to break

The struggle

Inward tussle

Between my triune parts

My flesh, my mind, my heart

They all compete

For the driver's seat

The leading role

Who should have

Complete control?

Neither

Although they are of me

Contrarily

Continuously

Fighting against me

Which implies that I must

Surrender them to You

Because apart from the Creator

Of All three

Each one fails to point me

In the right direction

Leading me further away from perfection

Down a long road of viewer discretion

Although

I've been advised

Zig-zags, U-Turns, and roundabouts

Cycles

Taking miracles

To get me out

When the path is straight and narrow

To stray or step away

Simply means I'm being misled

By my own self

Whether it be through

My spirit, my soul, or my flesh

Your Spirit is the **ONLY**

Reliable, accurate GPS

Father knows best

But it's up to me to follow

My will is free

But what I choose to do with it

Will always cost me

One way or another

There will be a price to pay

Some sort of sacrifice laid

Be it for gain

Or for loss

Depends on the chosen way

But One Turn towards You

All it takes to break

The struggle

Inward tussle

Not that there won't be trouble

But the benefits of **REPENTANCE**

Dismiss the ignorance

Of my wrong choices

A Tini Step

In the previous poem, "Still," we discussed the importance of sitting in the presence of God. Sometimes we run from this because of our lifestyle. We're too ashamed to face our Father. If we're lost in a life of sin and recklessness, chasing after our own prideful and lustful desires, we may not be comfortable seeking God, reading His Word, or listening to anything He may want to say to us. This causes us to avoid the very One whom we desperately need. He's the One who can save us from ourselves and restore us to where we need to be.

There are those who would make this more complicated than it is. Thinking, "I have to get my entire life together so that I can live for the Lord." On the contrary, one turn around is all there is to it. It's simple. Once you make the decision that you're fed up with the filth that comes with prodigal living, you turn around and away from the motive of self pleasing. The rest is a

process that is walked out one step at a time. Jesus'
death, burial, and resurrection was not for those who are
perfect in their own strength. He came for those of us
who mess up, and guess what, that's everybody!

Reread "Right This Way." Then answer the following
questions:

1. Have you been avoiding prayer and communion with
   God? If so, why?

   _____

   _____

   _____

   _____

   _____

   _____

2. Write out a prayer of confession of what you've done, asking for forgiveness and also wisdom and strength to make better decisions.

_____

_____

_____

_____

_____

_____

_____

_____

_____

_____

3. Find someone you trust who can pray with you and hold you accountable for your choices. What is the name of the person you've chosen and why did you choose him or her?

_____

_____

_____

_____

_____

_____

_____

_____

_____

_____

MOLD ME

In a world of instant gratification

We lack the patience

Needed for anything of quality

While still demanding quality

We don't want to wait

Or put in the work it takes

The audacity!

We want to have and to be better NOW

But demanding the end results

While refusing to start at the beginning

Or go through the middle...

Foolishness

Anything worth having, worth being

Is worth working for, worth waiting for

Life's proven this

Short cuts become deep wounds

Wanting too much too soon

Becoming consumed

In selfishness

A short cut to doom

Flowers can't bloom

Before seeds are planted and watered

Even after growth needing to be pruned

A painful part of the process when our character is groomed

But we can't stand the pain

Wanting sunshine without rain

Burn Out

How would the cake

Turn out

If all it did was bake?

There's a time and a season

For every rhyme

Every reason

But we just want what's pleasing

The enemy teasing

And tempting us to take the easy route

While God knows there's much in us

That needs to be weeded out

The Master Gardener

Divine Potter

Taking us from lumps of clay

Shaping us into beautiful vessels

His artwork being prepped for display

Taking His time

Using His hands

Kneading, Molding, Shaping, Smoothing

The Greatest of Artists work in this way

Mending the cracks and nicks

That come when we disobey

Go astray

Or simply forget to pray

Pushing and Pressing

The pain, a blessing

The Process a testing

A proving

Of who we will be

After going through it

Fire Consuming

Burning away the dross

To make the purest of gold

The heat necessary

To make us extraordinary

Customary

But we must NOT grow weary

Though we wait

The vision of who we really are may tarry

But don't faint

Or drown out the lesson of the Process

With complaint

For there's power in the testimony

Base word being **TEST**

This is **Growth** at its best...

A Tini Step

"Mold Me" is an interesting poem because it was written after I listened to an instrumental that was sent to me by a music producer. The track was so nice that the words flowed right out. The music producer, D. U. D. E., gave me the title and the track, and after spending time listening to it and writing the poem, I came to his studio and recorded it! It is a part of a project that is still being put together at the time of this writing. I look forward to hearing it once it is all complete. While this was my first time doing something like that, I believe that there will be more opportunities.

When D. U. D. E. gave me the title, immediately I began to think of the process of making pottery and other types of art. Any artist knows that it's not pretty until it is. Imagine being a lump of clay that is being transformed into a beautiful vase. The pressure, the time, it all leads to a beautiful ending. James 1:4 tells us that patience has a work which results in us being complete and without lack. The more advanced our society becomes, the less room it seems to have for patience. We have to constantly remind ourselves that works of great value just simply take time. God could have instantly created everything; however, He had specific days set aside for manifesting certain creations. If He was not in a rush, should we be?

Reread "Mold Me." Then answer the following questions:

1. Write about a time you had to wait awhile for something to happen, and you were so glad that you did.

   _____

   _____

   _____

   _____

   _____

2. In what area of your life are you currently having to practice patience? For what are you waiting and what will be the benefit of this patience?

_____

_____

_____

_____

_____

_____

_____

_____

_____

_____

_____

DECEPTIVE PERSPECTIVE

As I look at the situation

I instantly become overwhelmed

This is too much

Much greater than myself

As I stare into the eye of the storm

The winds churn

The view turns

Gray, more and more

All I see is destruction

Walls crashing

Windows bashing

The dysfunction of deconstruction

But what my eyes can't see

Is the miracle happening right before me

Or better yet, within me

A clearing

Starting a new project

What is old is being ripped away

My old mindset

Old way of doing things

Old habits...

None of it can stay

But I'm so blinded by the transition

That I don't quite see it that way

Eyes too filled with dismay

Once I stop crying about what I think I'm losing

I'll see the gain

And realize I can handle this pain

Finding less reason to complain

And more reason to embrace the process

Because on the other side of what seems a mess

Is a BETTER me

Regardless of what my eyes choose to see

I'll be much wiser, much stronger than I used to be

Or am currently

Greater than optimism is FAITH

I'll focus my gaze

On the outcome and away from

The temporary illusion of feeling outdone or overcome

For I am a CHOSEN one

Therefore, vision must override sight

Otherwise, I'll live my life

In constant fright

Mistaking just right

For all wrong

While He's waiting for me to sing a new song

One of the substance of things hoped for

Vision blurred no more

My **Deceptive Perspective** was like a closed door

Now unlocked by revelation

This overwhelming situation

With all its frustrations

Is viewed as elevation

But in order to move up

Some things must come down

Even if comfort didn't receive an invitation

I'll be patient

Being perfected

Although painstaking

Is so WORTH it

    Can you see it now?

A Tini Step

"Deceptive Perspective" is very similar to "Mold Me." They both discuss patience. However, "Deceptive Perspective" takes it a step or two further by addressing, not just the process, but how we perceive what is taking place. I have been in seasons of my life where I thought everything was out of control and falling apart. I actually wrote this poem in the middle of one. I sat down and began writing how I was feeling, and supernaturally, what I should've been thinking flowed out onto the paper.

Perhaps, the times we feel like our life is a complete mess are times life is actually "under construction." Proverbs 16:9 tells us that although we may have plans, the Lord orders our steps. This tells me that the way we decide a situation should go, just might not be how it all plays out. We have to be okay knowing by faith that it will all work out for our good. Don't let your sight blind you. Looks can and will definitely be deceiving. Think with eyes of faith.

Reread "Deceptive Perspective." Then answer the following questions:

1. Describe a tough season from your past. What happened?

_____

_____

_____

_____

_____

_____

_____

_____

_____

2. Looking back, was it as tough as it seemed while you were going through it?

_____

_____

_____

_____

_____

_____

3. What lessons did you learn from this season? What good came from it?

_____

_____

_____

_____

_____

_____

KEEP PRESSIN'

God is making a way

Rivers in the desert

My faith's trying to wither away

But I know I just can't let it

So I'll keep pressin'

Just keep pressin'

The devil may be busy

But God's Spirit don't sleep

And though I'm weak, I won't grow weary

'Cause I know He's working for me

So I'll keep pressin'

Just keep pressin'

A Breakthrough is coming

In my heart I believe it

They ask how I know for sure

By faith I receive it

So I'll keep pressin'

Just keep pressin'

He's leading me forward

I'll move in obedience

I can't stay here too long

Shake off the pain; It's just a feelin'

So I'll keep pressin'

Just keep pressin'

You keep pressin'

We'll keep pressin'

A Tini Step

Once I got past the realization of the tough season through which I was walking (the process described in "Deceptive Perspective"), I understood that I was going to have to just push my way through it. The season had an end. In my mind, I could visualize it, but I just wasn't there physically. This is how "Keep Pressin'" was birthed. To give some background about the situation, I taught in my local school district for twelve and a half years. The last year of those almost thirteen years, I could tell that a shift was taking place. It was more of an internal shift than anything.

Aspects of teaching that brought great joy, no longer did. Activities, during which I flowed in an abundance of grace, began to take more mental energy than they should, considering my track record. The more I prayed about it, the more I was uncomfortable with what I was sensing. What was my life without teaching kids in a classroom? I felt the pull to reset and refocus, to write and write only.

At the time of the writing of this book, all of this is pretty fresh and somewhat of a sensitive subject. However, for understanding purposes and despite vulnerability, I am sharing. There are far too many details to include in this book. The point is, after I became okay with the fact that I was about to walk away from what I had worked towards and in for over half of my life, getting to the end of the season was tough. With the end in mind, though, I managed.

It was obvious that my last school year was upon me. I didn't want to leave in the middle of the school year. I just couldn't do it. That being said, the time between December and May was awkwardly difficult. I wrote "Keep Pressin'" while strumming my mother's guitar and pouring out my heart. Singing the lyrics helped me press to the other side. It probably sounded like the most depressing and down in the dumps song ever sang, but it worked for me. I would sing it with tears flowing and walk through another day of teaching until there weren't any more.

Reread "Keep Pressin'." Then answer the following questions:

1. Describe a time in your life when you were ready to "throw in the towel" on something that you knew God wanted you to complete.

_____

_____

_____

_____

_____

_____

_____

_____

_____

2. If you did throw in the towel, are you able to pick it back up and finish what you started?

_____

_____

_____

_____

_____

3. Praying, writing, and singing are some of activities that help me press on and push through tough situations. What helps you?

_____

_____

_____

_____

_____

SURRENDER

I got tired of fighting against the current

Waters beating me like I stole something

I swam as hard and as fast as I could

Gave it everything I had within me

I'm just going to stop...

Stop swimming

Stop fighting

Stop trying to force it

I would say I'm giving up

But that sounds like it takes thought and effort

I don't have anything left to give

So how could it even be called that?

Exhaustion

Frustration

Overwhelming defeat

Let the waters take me

Wherever They lead

Because I can't do this anymore

I need REST

Will I float, sink, get washed up on an island?

The energy to care is not in me

It was diluted, eroded, washed away

So now I'll fall back and accept my fate

Wait...

All that fighting

You mean to tell me

I've had a life preserver on

This entire time?

A Tini Step

"Keep Pressin'" describes the time period immediately after I made the decision to quit my job as a teacher. However, "Surrender" illustrates the season that preceded that decision. There is a difference between pushing and pressing towards what God has shown you and fighting against His plan for you. The motive and purpose will let you know which one you're doing. I had to ask myself, "Why is this so difficult?" It was because I wasn't listening. I had felt that I would one day transition out of the classroom, but I didn't want to come to terms with even the idea that it would be so soon.

The fight continued. Even when I realized what was happening, I spent a few months in denial. The level of frustration inside of me was causing me more problems than necessary and was easily noticeable at times. Once I surrendered and declared that I would do what I felt in my heart I was being led to do, the process was not a walk in the park, but it had purpose. Purpose can help push you through any difficult season. Rebellion and stubbornness, on the other hand, are just a waste of time and energy. Prayer and meditation are the only way to know the difference between the two. God knows the plans He has for us. Those plans involve a purpose greater than ourselves (Jeremiah 29:11).

Reread "Surrender." Then answer the following questions:

1. Have you prayed about God's will and purpose for your life? What do you feel He's leading you to do in this season?

_____

_____

_____

_____

_____

2. Are you walking in those plans or are you fighting against them? How do you know?

_____

_____

_____

_____

_____

_____

_____

_____

_____

_____

_____

_____

BEAUTIFULLY BOLD

Like a fire breathing dragon

The words from your mouth

Can be hot enough to melt hearts

Not in a bad way

Or in a sad way

But in a way that speaks past

The masks

Or facades people tend to hide behind

And look through

Straight to the issue

At hand

No time for watering down

Or coats of sugar

Only sprinkles of grace

The seasoning that flavors

Every word you say

So fear not

Rise Up

Speak out

Louder than the doubt

You think the evil one wants

You to open your mouth?

Of course not

That's why there's opposition

Intimidation seeking to be

Counterproductive to your assigned mission

Oh...

But the Holy Spirit

Lives in you

With Power greater

Than any in this world

Trust and believe

The devil is afraid of you

He knows a thing or two

About what you were made to do

Give us the words

The Father gave to you

Words that cast out demons

End generational curses

Give comfort and confidence

Confirms callings and purposes

He is with you Speaking through you

As you **BOLDLY** declare

His revelation and wisdom

A weapon of mass CONstruction

Your mouth

So fear not

Rise up

Speak out

Louder than the doubt

A Tini Step

Boldness is a word that I feel gets misused often.
Working with children for over a decade has given me
access to so many personality types. Children who are
bossy, rude, and demanding of their own way are
mistaken for being bold, as if these are good qualities.
They even assume that these children will make great
leaders.

The boldness that I speak of in "Beautifully Bold"
does not fit that description. Scriptural boldness is
coupled with righteousness (Proverbs 28:1) and
confidence in the Lord (2 Corinthians 3:11-12). The
person who is the inspiration behind this piece was known
for both. I say "was" because she is no longer with us on
Earth. This poem was written soon after she transitioned.
My memories of her are filled with words that pierced
my heart in a way that could only have come from the
Lord, Himself by way of the Holy Spirit. A quality of

Marta's that I have always admired. THIS is true boldness!

While Marta's words may not have been what I wanted to hear in that moment, they were always what I needed. I never perceived them as rude or bossy because I am able to discern God's words and His grace. We are told to come BOLDLY to God with our requests (Hebrews 4:16). Why would we ever think that it would mean to be rude, inconsiderate, and/or forceful? The thought alone feels disrespectful. Between Hebrews 12:14-15, Colossians 4:6, and Ephesians 4:29, the Word clearly expresses that boldness does not give us a license to go around "telling folks off." We are to, on the contrary, use our words to build people up, shed light in areas of darkness, and rebuke the works of the enemy for the sake of salvation.

Reread "Beautifully Bold." Then answer the following questions:

1. Describe a time when someone was bold enough to use their words to help build you up and a time when someone's words did the opposite. Compare the two scenarios. How did you feel? What were the benefits or issues?

_____

_____

_____

_____

_____

_____

_____

_____

_____

_____

2. Does this poem remind you of anyone? If so, who
   and how so? (Be sure to reach out to that person
   or those people if you are still able, and thank
   them for their boldness.)

_____

_____

_____

_____

_____

_____

_____

_____

_____

FRIEND TO THE FRIENDLESS

I saw you sitting by yourself

So I grabbed a seat

You looked lost on your journey

So I helped you seek

This lonely road appeared longer than life

On the contrary

Maybe the road's not long enough

A friend helps fine tune your perspective

Time flies when it's shared with someone

Especially when for so long

You felt you had no one

Outcast or outlier

Either way

On the outside of together

Looking in

Wondering whether

Anyone sees you

I do

It appeared as if I came out of nowhere

Just in time

For your moment of despair

Felt like too much to bear

So you chose not to share

And who could you dare tell

If no one cares

But I do

I'm on assignment

Like a secret agent

Sent to sit beside

Walk along with

Listen and encourage

Uplift

Help carry the load

Whatever's needed in this moment

Your low season

Where you couldn't even

Articulate what you needed

But Divine Intervention

Spiritual Intuition

Interceded

As I did that which I was created to do

Your answered prayer

Because He hears

He cares

He loves you

Therefore, He sent me to be

What I've often needed

    A Friend to the Friendless

A Tini Step

"Beautifully Bold" and "Friend of the Friendless" are both near and dear to my heart because they were written in memory of friends who are no longer with us. I was asked by a friend and mentor of mine to write a poem about being a "friend to the friendless" after I used those words to describe myself. I didn't realize at the time that our mutual friend had those same words written in her eulogy. She had been fighting cancer for a while and had her services planned just in case.

I wasn't able to write the poem at first because I was thinking about myself. It felt weird to me. While sitting in Brandy's funeral listening to her eulogy being read, I heard these words, "She was a friend to the friendless." My eyes widened and tears flowed. I had no idea! After a period of grieving, I realized what I needed to do. I had to write this poem. It not only pulled me out of a funk, but it also brought me great joy to have known her.

Proverbs 18:24 reminds us that if we want friends
we must be friendly. Brandy definitely had lots of
friends, and she was probably the friendliest, goofiest
person out of everyone I've ever known, myself included.
Her boldness was different from Marta's but both types
are needed. She was bold enough to be herself. Bold
enough to befriend anyone, even those that some would
shun. Although we've known each other for years, she
and I were not friends that hung out a lot or even talked
often until the spring of 2020 when it seemed the whole
world shut down. God has a great way of bringing people
along for such a time.

Reread "Friend to the Friendless." Then answer the
following questions:

1. Is there someone you've noticed may need your friendship? Who is this person? What small things can you do for him or her to be a person of joy in his or her life?

_____

_____

_____

_____

2. Does this poem remind you of anyone? If so, who and how so? (Be sure to reach out to that person or those people if you are still able and thank them for their friendliness or friendship.)

_____

_____

_____

_____

KID AT HEART

There's a place I used to live

I resided there for a while

A joyfully free place

Where flowers had a strong smell

As if they grew straight from your nose

And grass was greener there

I suppose

The smiles and laughs

Couldn't be contained

Not in this place

Fun in the sun

Skipping in the rain

Every season gave reason to dance

There were troubles there, yes

 But the sting of them never lasted long

Like a bee dying immediately afterwards

I lived in this place as long as I could

But I was forced into exile

Oceans away

Shipped to a place of total contrast

To a land where volcanoes of laughter and smiles

Don't easily erupt

And when they do

It's just used as a mask or make up

To cover up

That everyone longs to return to our old home

Because here we're surrounded by people

But still all alone

There we made company all on our own

Playing with members of our imaginations

While still knowing how to give real people an invitation

Into our world

Instead of aching for that place

Walking around with a discontented heart

And a painted on happy face

I've learned how to make internal visits

Being just as unrestrained

As the child I remember

Hopeful

Inviting

Imaginative

Full of Wonder

Oh how sweet it is to be

A Kid at Heart

A Tini Step

I love this poem! I'm not just saying that because I wrote it. It's because of the reminder to let go of burdens and hold on to freedom. Being an adult often gets a bad rap. Yes, there are more responsibilities and pressures for an adult than children experience. Between bills, jobs, families, and numerous other daunting tasks that I care not to even try to list, life is far from easy. While at the time of writing this I do not have any children of my own, I have and continue to spend enough time with a great number of them to know that we can learn many valuable lessons from them.

I'm definitely not saying that you should ignore all responsibilities, depend solely on your parents, and drop on the floor pouting whenever you don't get your way. First Corinthians 13:11 tells us to grow up and put away childish things. This verse comes immediately after a thorough description of love and is eventually followed by the words "but the greatest of these is love" (NKJV). Children can be extremely selfish and egocentric. They also lack discipline. "It's all about me!" As we are growing and maturing in our walk with God, we should be growing and maturing in our ability to love and in our discipline.

Despite having a tough time loving, sharing, and carrying out responsibilities, what children excel at is trusting and believing. They have a carefree nature about them that we adults struggle to grasp. I'm sure the bills and all those other items mentioned earlier have much to do with it, but this does not excuse us. Matthew 10: 13-16 and 18:3-4, Luke 18:17, and 1 Peter 2:2 all speak to childlike faith. As children trust and rest in the belief that their parents will take good care of them, we should trust and rest that God is doing just that for us. It's all about faith.

True faith has no room for worries. True faith allows the joy of the Lord to strengthen in times of weakness. When you feel yourself becoming overwhelmed with life, visualize a child playing outside while their parents are taking care of business. Trust that as you are taking care of business, God is taking care of you.

Reread "Kid at Heart." Then answer the following questions:

1. Have the cares of this world, the burdens of life, and the list of your daily obligations caused you to lose sight of joy and peace? If so, how can you tell? What is different about you?

_____

_____

_____

_____

_____

_____

_____

2. Find scriptures about joy, and write out the one that really speaks to your heart on an index card. Place the card somewhere in your home where you will frequently see it. Which scripture did you choose?

_____

_____

_____

_____

_____

_____

_____

_____

_____

_____

3. Write out a sincere prayer to God about where you are spiritually and mentally and ask Him to help guide you to where you desire to be. Let your chosen scripture be the foundation of your prayer

_____

_____

_____

_____

_____

_____

_____

_____

_____

_____

TO THIS DAY

I still hope

A simple yet profound statement

I STILL HOPE

Despite the hardships, failures, and letdowns

I've encountered

I still hope

I don't even know why I felt

The need to write these words

But as soon as my pen hit the paper

They flowed from it

I

(Me, myself)

Still

(To this day, to this moment)

Hope

(Believe that better is not only on its way

But that it already arrived

And has begun to get settled in)

It's only a matter of patience

Because time is brutal without patience

Patience rests in **HOPE**

Not a "might as well" type of hope

But a hope that curls the edges

Of my mouth

Slowly but surely

Upward

A smile that arises

From a deep place

An unexplainable but very real place

One decorated with the words

"I'm working

Trust Me

This too shall pass

I know the plans

I have for you"

These words cover the walls

Of this place

Like captivating graffiti

On a building

Marked territory

I've said all this to say

I STILL HOPE

Do you?

You should

A Tini Step

I sat down in a college library one afternoon, determined to write. As soon as I opened my notebook, these words were written without hesitation. Apparently I was feeling pretty positive that day. "To This Day" and "Kid at Heart" both speak to the spark that tends to fade as life's demands and disappointments erode us mentally, physically, and spiritually.

At the time of writing this, I am 37 and have yet to bear a child or be married. Some would say that I should not be bothered with the thought of ever doing either at my age, but as the writing states, "I still hope." Not just for these things to manifest in my life, but for numerous "crazy" dreams. As tough as life has been (when has life not been tough on some level), one aspect of my being that I have managed to preserve is a hope for better. As a child and adolescent, I would have called this optimism, but as I have grown, matured, and developed a relationship with the Lord, I've traded the optimism for true hope and faith.

There were a few times in my earlier years where I was on the edge of my hope and teetering into hopelessness, but right when I was about to give it all up, God sent someone or something to help stand me up before I fell over. Now, I make it my business to do the same for others I encounter, to be a person of hope, to reignite the flame in them before it dwindles too low. Considering the many who have done it for me, it is my duty and privilege.

Reread "To This Day." Then answer the following questions:

1. Is there an area of your life you feel you're beginning to or have already seen your hope wither away? In what area, and what caused this hopelessness?

_____

_____

_____

_____

_____

2. I dare you to dream and hope again. Write out a list of requests that you hope God will answer. Pray over them. Believe for them

_____

_____

_____

_____

Other books by

Martinis Stephens:

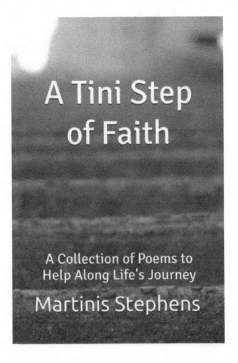